NUNCHAKU IN ACTION
For Kobudo and Law Enforcement

by
JOSEPH C. HESS
Chief Instructor
Broward County Police Academy

Editor: Gregory Lee
Graphic Design: Karen Massad

Art Production:
Mary Schepis, Dung Pham

Eighth printing 1998

OHARA  PUBLICATIONS, INCORPORATED
SANTA CLARITA, CALIFORNIA

DEDICATION

I wish to dedicate this book to master Ed Verycken for the influence and help he has given me throughout my martial arts life, and for his untiring hours of weapons training.

Special thanks to Ron Russell and Joe Kelljchian for their devoted time and help in making this book possible.

ABOUT THE AUTHOR

Joseph Hess is considered one of the finest martial arts and police-training instructors in the country. He has personally been responsible for 17 black belt instructors who are currently teaching nationally. He holds a tenth degree black belt in goju-ryu karate, a fourth degree black belt in Okinawan karate, and a red sash in the northern system of gung fu. He also holds rankings in judo, aikijitsu and jujitsu.

Hess was the world heavyweight champion in full-contact karate from 1975-77. As a result, he has been featured in over 60 different magazine and newspaper articles, and has appeared on many local, national and international television programs, including ABC's *Wide World of Sports*. In addition, he is the author of numerous articles on physical fitness for police officers, and has written three books dealing with defensive tactics and stick fighting.

Hess is currently the chief instructor in physical training and unarmed defense for the Broward County Police Academy in Florida where he has been teaching for the past eight years. He has also traveled to South and Central America where he has trained law enforcement agencies throughout Ecuador and Mexico. A specialist in 16 different weapons, Hess teaches classes for black belts only in the use of these weapons.

Hess' first book, *Night Stick*, was published by Ohara in 1982.

PUBLISHER'S NOTE

This book was conceived by Joseph Hess to give all instructors of the martial arts a better understanding of how to teach the nunchaku as a tool for kata and as an effective self-defense weapon. It was also designed for advanced training in law enforcement work. Police departments who have found the nunchaku to be a valuable alternative to the traditional night stick will find this a thorough manual for instruction in this ancient weapon.

Hess has perfected his training course for the past dozen years, instructing more than 300 law enforcement agencies both in the U.S. and in Central America in the use of the nunchaku. The essentials of nunchaku handling and training are outlined, and Hess has included a wealth of self-defense situations and a special section on his own recommended workout for students who are serious about nunchaku training.

There is also a sample page of Hess' own task performance evaluation that is a guideline for instructors on grading a student's performance and suggesting ways for improvement. It is one method of judging a student's progress in kobudo training. The rules and methods laid down in this book are not engraved in stone, but Hess has found through his many years of law enforcement work that many traditional techniques of the nunchaku will not necessarily be effective in all situations on the street, and therefore has devised some of his own applications of weapon handling.

Instructors particularly may want to alter some aspects of the training outlined here. We remind you only that this manual illustrates how Hess has effectively taught nunchaku handling to hundreds of law enforcement agencies and his own black belts.

As a final note, please study carefully the illustrations and text before attempting any of the basic motions and self-defense techniques. It is for your own safety as well as for any partner working with you. The nunchaku is a serious weapon and often illegal to possess in certain states. Those who want to learn this weapon must have serious intentions and must respect the weapon and others who use it. The nunchaku can be an advanced path along the way of martial arts training, a new discipline for a student's body and mind. That is appropriate, for the nunchaku has for centuries been a very effective tool of the Okinawan karate systems.

INTRODUCTION

At first glance one might think that the nunchaku is merely a bundle of sticks tied together with a piece of rope or string. To the unsuspecting attacker, however, this weapon is akin to an unleashed tiger, leaping to deliver one swift strike. Once a farm implement used for threshing grain by the indigenous people of Okinawa, the nunchaku has become a weapon surrounded by controversy. Considered by many states as a deadly weapon, illegal to possess, the nunchaku has many nicknames: chucks, speed sticks, nutcracker, flail, swing sticks.

Rules and regulations need to be established by qualified martial arts instructors and police departments to standardize the use of the nunchaku. Too many instructors introduce their students to the nunchaku before they are ready, teaching this weapon to beginners to retain their interest in the martial arts and curb the dropout rate. This is improper and irresponsible. If one is a dedicated student of the martial arts, he or she will have plenty of time to find out about the nunchaku. Unfortunately, martial arts movies have given this weapon a lot of publicity, and tend to show this weapon giving users superhuman ability. Defeating an opponent is not the sole purpose of the nunchaku. It is an ancient weapon that can reveal to the serious martial artist better uses for his body, a source of inspiration for kata and a dynamic tool for improving his martial arts training

The clear advantage of the nunchaku in police work is its unequaled ability to block any attack and then instantly be converted for use as a come-along tool—a suspect in the pinch of a nunchaku hold has no choice but to "come along."

When closed, the nunchaku can be used in very close quarters, or if extended, it has a reach several inches more than the standard patrolman's night stick. Spun about the body, it can keep opponents from getting too close. A policeman who knows the nunchaku intimately will have more confidence and will be less likely to rely on his service revolver to end a hostile situation, nor will he necessarily need to break bones with the weapon. With its multiplicity of holds and takedown techniques, the nunchaku is ideal for self-defense without resorting to deadly force.

To list some of the advantages of the nunchaku:
- It has a speed ratio that is seven times faster than a night stick.
- When closed, it can be carried easily in the back pocket.

- When in motion, it is nearly impossible to grab and take away.
- It exerts a great deal of pressure when used in a come-along hold—up to 150 pounds per square inch.
- An assailant can be struck even when he's directly behind you.
- The ridges can cause extreme, incapacitating pain.
- Blocks can be delivered in two places at the same time.
- Constant practice improves quickness and confidence.

Some disadvantages of the weapon are:
- The nunchaku requires more practice than any other weapon.
- If untrained, a person trying to use a nunchaku may cause more harm to himself than to an attacker.
- The centrifugal force of the nunchaku sticks when spun in motion can easily break bones.
- If not checked regularly for wear, the string or cord can break, causing the sticks to fly out of control.
- Without practice on a heavy punching bag, the recoil affect of the weapon can cause injury to one's fingers, elbows, face, knees, etc.
- Use of the nunchaku is often illegal (depending on the state) and can bring on lawsuits.

For law enforcement officers, some of the dos and don'ts of nunchaku training are:
- Avoid head contact.
- Use only when all other means of compliance have failed.
- Strike bone areas first.
- Do not strike drugged or intoxicated persons.
- Use as a come-along tool first—a striking tool last.
- Keep the nunchaku locked up when off duty.
- Never "show off" or demonstrate with them, and never give the nunchaku to anyone.
- Check it periodically for wear, frayed string or rough edges.

During my two decades of martial arts training, and my dozen years in law enforcement, I have seen many weapons come and go. The nunchaku is one weapon that will never lose its effectiveness. After training more than 300 law enforcement agencies, dozens of black belts and many government agencies, I feel that for those who know the capabilities of the nunchaku and who respect its tradition, they have an unbeatable combination for self-defense.

—Joseph C. Hess
Fort Lauderdale, Florida
February, 1983

PERFORMANCE OBJECTIVES

ACTIVITY TASK SHEET

ACTIVITY or DRILL EVALUATION OF TECHNIQUE	INSTRUCTOR RATING					
	Good		Fair		Poor	
	L	R	L	R	L	R
1.						
2.						
3.						
4.						
5.						
6.						
7.						
8.						
9.						
10.						
COMMENTS:						

When evaluating a student's ability with the nunchaku, I use a task sheet like the one pictured above. This performance activity task sheet should be filled in by each instructor to keep a running report on the student's progress after each technique, drill, exercise, or defense technique. The student will be watched carefully by the instructor and given ten times to display his proficiency. At the bottom of the sheet is a place for the instructor's comments, which will aid the student and let him know where he is the weakest. At the top under your rating scale you will also see "L" for Left Hand and "R" for Right Hand. Under evaluation of technique you should write good points or bad points that the student makes when working with the nunchaku.

TYPES OF NUNCHAKU

ROUNDED NUNCHAKU
This is the popular street model, and is not as effective for control work, only for long- and short-distance blocking and striking.

RUBBER PRACTICE NUNCHAKU
Ideal for the novice when first learning how to handle the nunchaku. It allows practice without injury to a partner or oneself. This is not good for working out on a heavy bag. Also constant pressure will break the top of this weapon.

RIDGED NUNCHAKU
Best type for police work because of the effectiveness of the ridged edges which can cause great pain when used for pinch holds and strikes. It is an excellent come-along tool.

CONTENTS

WARM-UPS

When doing these warm-up exercises remember to always use your weapon with each exercise. This will test the strength of the nunchaku string as you perform each of these isometric pulls. If the weapon is going to break, it will break now rather than during your practice workout.

WARM-UP EXERCISES:
1. Horizontal Pull (Low)
2. Overhead Pull (Standing)
3. Vertical Side Pull (Left and Right)
4. Back Pull (Down)
5. Back Pull (Up)
6. Back Pull (Outward)
7. Overhead Pull (Seated)
8. Forward Pull
9. Squat Pull

HORIZONTAL PULL (Low)

Keeping a firm grip on the nunchaku, try to pull it apart. Hold for about ten seconds and repeat a total of five times. These exercises will build up strength in your wrists and arms, as well as firm your natural grip.

OVERHEAD PULL
(Standing)

Extend the nunchaku overhead and repeat the same outward pull against the center of the nunchaku. Repeat five times, holding each pull a total of ten seconds.

VERTICAL SIDE PULL
(Left and Right)

Bending in a side position helps build up the side muscles and shoulders. It will aid you in case it is necessary to deliver a block in this manner. Make sure that the lower hand is pulling downward and the higher hand is pulling upward while staying in this side bent position. You may want to keep your body in constant motion, swinging gently overhead from right to left, back and forth, maintaining a constant pull on the nunchaku.

BACK PULL (Down)

This pull and the next are quite similar. To develop the upper arms and shoulders, rest the upper hand on the back of the shoulder and pull with the lower hand downward, increasing the pressure in the shoulder area. Repeat this pull on the left side (left hand high, right hand low). Be careful when you release your grip on the sticks while changing sides as a lot of tension is generated with these isometric pulls.

BACK PULL (Up)

To switch to an upward pull, simply raise your upper arm higher but maintain a steady pulling motion with the lower hand. Hold each pull about ten seconds and repeat this pull at least four times before switching to your other shoulder. You may find in doing these exercises that one arm is considerably weaker than the other and should be exercised more.

BACK PULL (Outward)

Excellent for the fingers and wrists. Notice that the hands are now palms forward. The pulling motion is outward with a wide stance. Try to extend your arms away from your body at least ten inches. For an extra workout, try bending at the knees and touching the ground behind you. For further benefits, start to bend your upper body forward, while maintaining a constant pull on the weapon.

OVERHEAD PULL
(Seated)

From a seated position, pull the sticks outward over your head. This pull may be done while raising the feet together off the ground to benefit stomach muscles, or placed on the ground while leaning backward at a 45-degree angle to strengthen your back. Repeat.

FORWARD PULL

Try to place the center string of the nunchaku over your extended foot (1) while still grasping the weapon with both hands. After placing the weapon over the foot, try to pull yourself forward (2), bending the back at the waist and not just bending your head. Your goal should be to touch your forehead on either kneecap. Repeat with the other leg.

SQUAT PULL
(For Two Persons)

One person should hold the outside of the nunchaku sticks while the other person holds the inside of the weapon. Staying in a squat position, try to move about (1) and pull the weapon out of the hands of the other person. Try to upset the other person's balance while trying to maintain yours and keep from falling. Alternate grasping the weapon on the inside and then the outside. If you feel your partner starting to lose his balance, try yanking the weapon upward (2) with a quick motion to make him let go. This exercise is quite challenging—and amusing—if done with eyes closed.

READY POSITIONS

The following ready positions and stances show the proper ways to hold the nunchaku in preparing to execute the defensive techniques outlined in this book. Though these stances are only maintained for brief periods, it is important that they be memorized in training until they are a natural part of your responses to real-life situations. Assume these ready positions each time you practice any technique.

READY POSITIONS:
1. High Point (Short Guard)
2. Low Point (Short Guard)
3. Shoulder Load
4. Rear (Lower Back)
5. Rear (45-Degree Angle)
6. Front Load
7. Side Trap
8. Forearm
9. Neck
10. Underarm
11. Side Overhead

SHORT GUARD / OPEN STICK

Anytime the weapon is held in the closed position, it is referred to as a short guard position. Anytime the sticks are held in a separated position, it is referred to as an open stick position.

HIGH POINT READY POSITION

This is a short guard position held across the chest. Blocks and strikes can be made quickly from this ready position with little warning. The string end is at the top and the grip is inward, palms facing your body. If you are left-handed, you would have your left hand in the low point or bottom position. If right-handed, your right hand should be lowest.

LOW POINT READY POSITION

The weapon is held low in one hand and close to your body, with the stance slightly wider and your catch (alternate) hand ready to block or counter an opponent. Your palm is facing the opponent, with the sticks held near the base and angled toward the ground.

SHOULDER LOAD READY POSITION

This side load ready position is one of the best ''non-agressive'' ready stances to assume. It affords a great deal of protection to both front and side, and allows you to strike with either hand. In this case, the left hand can strike an attacker's upper body, while the right hand can strike out at the legs. The position appears very relaxed, with no indication that a strike can be made swiftly.

REAR READY POSITION
(Lower Back)

When this position is viewed from the front, one might not see the nunchaku. A very good position if you want your attacker to think you are unarmed. From this point, you can strike with either hand and be able to recover quickly to the same position. The weapon is held very close to the body and the hands will tend to conceal the ends of the sticks. The palms of both hands should face inward toward your body.

REAR READY POSITION
(45-Degree Angle)

This position allows you a choice of striking moves, and the weapon can be used to block a strike directed toward your back from the rear. Your strong hand should be holding the top stick so that you can deliver a powerful blow with a downward stroke.

FRONT READY POSITION

This open stick position is ideal for preparing for a direct frontal assault, whether it be a kick, punch or knife attack. The sticks should be held about chest high, with hands close to the bottom of each stick to afford maximum blocking or striking power in any direction. It also allows you to move quickly into any other ready position. Try to keep the weapon out away from your body, but don't let an attacker reach out and grab the weapon from you.

SIDE TRAP READY POSITION

This is a good stable position for striking which allows you to move but does not restrict your striking moves. By "trapping" the weapon you are able to either grab with the trap hand and strike or use the forward hand to lash out with. This position is effective for trapping the nunchaku if a horizontal strike has missed your attacker and you need to stop the swing of the nunchaku quickly.

FOREARM READY POSITION

A quick position to assume. It allows you to block with the front stick across your forearm and deliver a strike with the rear stick (held here in the right hand). The easiest way to move into this position is from the front ready position.

NECK READY POSITION

This position creates the impression that you are off guard with your arms crossed in front of you. But the nunchaku can be taken off the back of your neck swiftly and used to deliver a snap strike to either side of an opponent's body. In this example, the left arm should deliver the strike, as it is positioned over the right arm. A strike using the right arm would take a split second too long. Notice that the palms face inward and the nunchaku is held close to the neck. When you are ready to strike, your other hand must release its grip.

UNDERARM READY POSITION

One of the fastest ready positions for strike and recovery. It enables you to deliver a quick strike and then return the weapon to the underarm position. This is excellent for a knife attack from the front. Notice that your free hand is held high and close to the body, if you need to push or grab your opponent. The stick is held in the middle for greater speed while the other one is high and pinned under the armpit.

SIDE OVERHEAD READY POSITION

Strong horizontal, vertical or cross-X strikes can be delivered from this position. You can swing the nunchaku in a whipping motion that generates an awesome amount of speed. Notice that the palm faces outward and one end of the nunchaku is allowed to swing free. Keep your arm above your shoulder with a slight bend in your elbow. Keep your free hand in the center of your body for protection.

STICK PRACTICE

T he following stick movements and basic catches should be performed very slowly at first, so that you will begin to get a general understanding of how the weapon moves and its attitude while in motion. Remember, you must practice each of these exercises repeatedly with both hands so that one hand does not become any less coordinated with the nunchaku than the other. When you have done these exercises many times during training, the speeds and swinging motions of the weapon will become much more familiar, and you will have a lot more confidence in the nunchaku itself.

Always practice these movements in a large open area and make sure that you are well away from other people. Be sure particularly to check that there is no one standing too close behind you while you are practicing.

LEG FEED

This exercise is good for timing and coordination. (1) The right leg is lifted and the left hand, holding one stick of the nunchaku, passes the weapon underneath the right leg (2), feeding it to the right hand. Repeat this going the other way (3&4), with the right hand passing the weapon under-

neath the left leg to the left hand, back and forth. Continue for about three minutes, and catch the *same* stick you are holding, and not the stick that swings freely underneath. This exercise must be done without hitting your feet.

ONE STICK RELEASE

(1) From a short guard (sticks closed) position, it is necessary to practice releasing one stick and letting it swing forward (2) while maintaining your grip on the stick still in your hand. This permits you to open the weapon into a swing strike to the upper body, joints or groin and then retrieve the weapon (3) by parting your thumb and first finger and catching the stick as it returns. You must learn to time the catch so that you do not injure your fingers. Releasing the weapon is also tricky, because you must maintain your grip or lose the nunchaku entirely.

FINGER CATCH

(A) After throwing the nunchaku stick forward, you may catch it in one of two ways. The finger catch brings the weapon between the forefinger, while the other stick remains grasped in between the thumb and the other two fingers of your hand. This is a silent way to retrieve the weapon, and it is great for building up the fingers, but it is also painful at first until you get used to performing this catch.

CHANNEL CATCH

(B) A more natural way to catch the swinging portion of the nunchaku is to catch it in the same manner as it was released, that is, between the thumb and forefinger, allowing more control over the speed of the weapon. This is noisier than the finger catch, but also less painful.

2

3

A

B

1

FRONT CATCH

The ready position for the front catch is the short guard (1) high point position. Hold the weapon in your strong hand (in this case, the right hand) and prepare to step backward with the right foot (establishing a good ready position with your weight distributed evenly). As you step backward, throw the nunchaku (2) over your right shoulder and catch (3) the free end of the weapon in your left hand by reaching across the front of your chest. Try to time the stick and the hand together so that you catch it exactly at the final front catch position as shown here. (Note: Do *not* let go of the stick in the right hand.) This basic catch is not as easy at first as it looks. Now repeat this exercise on the left side, throwing the nunchaku stick over your left shoulder with your left hand and catching it in your right hand. This catch may serve simultaneously as a strike when your opponent is directly in front of you.

2

3

REAR CATCH

Begin the rear catch exercise in the same way as the front catch, that is, by throwing the nunchaku over your right shoulder (1) from a short guard, high point position. In this case, bring your catch hand behind you and against the small of the back (2) and let the stick meet your hand there (3) —do *not* try and move your hand about to meet the stick. If you practice placing your hand in the same spot every time, you will establish a good reference point. Be sure that when you catch the stick that both hands grasp the nunchaku tightly. This movement can allow you to strike an attacker either directly in front or in back of you.

FRONT CATCH EXERCISE
(Alternate)

This is a front catch and a strike at the same time. Perform the front catch as before (1-3), only this time, do not stop but immediately use your catch hand to throw the nunchaku over the opposite shoulder and perform a front catch (4-7) on the other side. Once you can switch hands back and forth without stopping, try to pick up a little speed and continue doing this exercise for at least two minutes. This exercise is excellent for timing and coordination. These exercises will also help you become familiar with the speed of the nunchaku and how to become accustomed to its movements without hitting yourself in the process.

REAR CATCH EXERCISE (Alternate)

This is the same as the front catch drill, merely repeating a rear catch over and over, exchanging the nunchaku from shoulder to shoulder. The stick is thrown (1) over the right shoulder and the left hand catches the stick (2) in the small of your back. Then the catch hand becomes the throwing hand (3) and you bring the stick around in front of you and throw it over your left shoulder. The right hand is now the

catch hand and grasps the nunchaku (4) in the same way. Practice this catch exchange until you can pick up some speed and repeat it for two minutes without stopping. When you have become more proficient in these catches, try doing the same drill with your eyes closed. This will help you build confidence in your ability to handle the nunchaku.

OUTSIDE CIRCLE EXERCISE

From a comfortable stance with the nunchaku open in one hand at your side begin to move your arm (1) in a clockwise motion, bringing it forward and up, then down and around (2-6) to the starting position. As your arm moves rapidly through this circle, spin the free stick with a slight motion of the wrist, twirling the stick like a helicopter blade. You now have two circles in motion, your arm describing an outside circle, and the stick circling inside. Keep this up continuously for two minutes, spinning the stick rapidly. Be sure to repeat this exercise with the other hand. Be careful not to strike yourself while the sticks are in motion.

2

3

5

6

SIDE LOAD EXERCISE

This block enables you to counter a strike from the side. From a front ready position (1), take your right hand and bring it in toward your chest and up (2&3), (as if you were executing an uppercut strike with your fist) while bringing your left hand down toward your right side into the shoulder load position. Keep the upper half of the nunchaku angled at 45 degrees to deflect any strikes. Now exchange the sticks into a left shoulder load position (4-8) by reversing the motions, bringing your right hand down inside your left arm and then moving your left arm inside and up, your right arm down and across. Repeat these movements back and forth until your technique builds up speed.

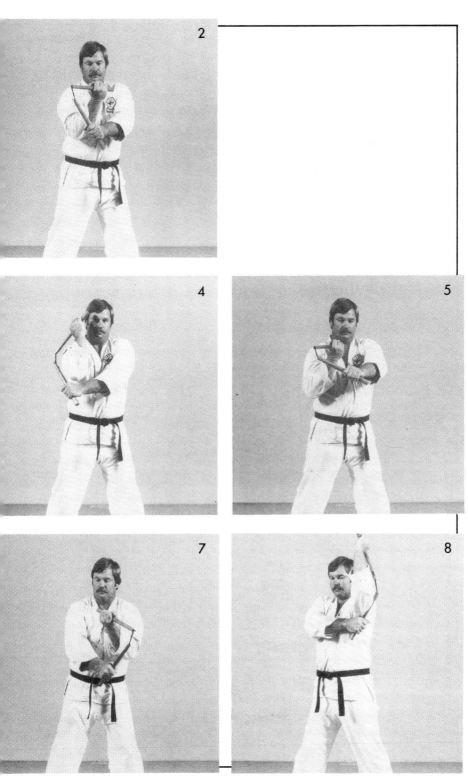

FRONT LOAD EXERCISE
(Alternate)

This load drill is almost identical to the previous load block, except that from a front ready position (1), after you have brought your right arm up inside your left arm (2) in the uppercut motion, keep the elbow of your right arm (3) positioned on top of your left arm and stick. The sticks should still be at a

45-degree angle to deflect strikes, but now the weapon is not on top of the shoulder but angled toward the front. To exchange, reverse the motions (4-6) by bringing your right arm down and across to the lower left side, your left arm up and inside, locking your left elbow on top of your right hand.

TRAPPING

Learning to trap the weapon and getting it under control is especially important when you consider that with the nunchaku you can generate a speed of 150 m.p.h. The side cover trap is the best way to contain the nunchaku after you have made a strike or have swung and missed your target. The trap allows you to prepare for another strike from another ready position. Practice swinging the weapon horizontally (1&2) in front of you and then trapping it with your palm (3) against your side. The object is not to smash the weapon against your side but to stop it from swinging with a last-minute braking motion with the wrist. After trapping it, use the opposite palm (the one you trapped the stick with) to grasp and swing the nunchaku out and around to trap it against the opposite side using the opposite hand. You should not try this exercise until you are more familiar with the speed of the weapon.

2

3

FLIP AND CATCH EXERCISE

Begin this exercise by swinging the nunchaku freely from one hand and then transferring it (1-4) to the opposite hand, back and forth, swinging the stick out in a circle (5-10) and then catching the free stick in your other hand. Try circling the stick several times in one hand before catching it in the opposite hand. This will help your timing and speed. Now try this drill with your eyes closed.

7

8

REVERSE FRONT CATCH

Try this alternate of the front catch only after you are familiar with the attitude and speed of the nunchaku, and begin very slowly. Notice that in this variation, the left hand throws the nunchaku *under* the right shoulder (1) and the swinging end of the weapon is now caught with the right hand (2) on top. The right hand now brings the weapon down and across the front of your body (3&4) and underneath the left shoulder into the left hand (5&6). One advantage of this technique is if you happen to miss a forward down strike at your attacker, where the weapon may be moving too quickly for you to stop it in any other way except behind your shoulder. When you have caught the weapon (as in 2 and 6), you are now in a shoulder load position, ready to strike or block again. Make sure you keep the weapon outside your upper arm. If you don't the sticks may strike the back of your head.

NECK CATCH EXERCISE

This drill must be practiced with extreme caution. Start by holding one stick in the right hand (1) and throw the weapon over the opposite shoulder and around the neck (2-4) catching the other end of the nunchaku with your left hand. Your throwing hand should maintain its grip on the nunchaku at all times, placed against your body and close to the side of your neck. The catch hand will be on the outside, in front of your right forearm. Now release the nunchaku with your right hand (5) and use the left hand to swing it out and back (6-8) across your right shoulder, repeating the catch with the right hand now outside your left (9&10) to make the catch.

7

8

BLOCKING

After practicing on a regular basis, your nunchaku skills will become very polished. Knowing how to avoid a strike without a harsh counterattack is desirable but not as easy as it sounds. You will have to learn a combination of stances and stick skills before you can come out of a real street attack.

A unique advantage of the nunchaku is that you can actually block two areas at the same time when the sticks are open. And any block can be immediately converted into a takedown technique which can enclose an attacker's wrist, arm or ankle in a vise-like grip exerting up to 150 pounds per square inch of pressure.

When blocking, always remember to execute with a snapping motion, recovering the weapon quickly to avoid having your opponent grab it and try to take it away from you. A swift block with the ridged nunchaku will be just as effective as a strike; in many cases, they are one and the same.

CLOSED STICK
SNAP BLOCK
(Inside of Leg)

(1) As your attacker throws a kick at you, step away from the direction of his kick (2) and deliver a sharp snap strike (3) to the shin area. Keep the free hand high and prepare for a follow up strike if necessary. The shin, like the wrist, is a very sensitive area when struck hard with the edge of a nunchaku stick.

CLOSED STICK
SNAP BLOCK
(Outside of Leg)

The snap block against a kick may also be executed to the outside of the attacker's kick, stepping away from the direction of the kick (1&2) as before and delivering a sharp blow (3) near the protruding bones of the foot, if possible, or even a downward strike to the top of the toes. When your opponent places his foot back on the ground, as he must, be prepared to follow up with another strike while he is off balance.

OPEN STICK BLOCK
(Inside of Leg)

An open stick block will not cause your attacker as much pain as a closed stick snap block, but you will have a great deal of protection and can pin the attacker's leg between the nunchaku sticks. (1) As a kick is thrown at you, shift away from the direction of the attack (2), opening the sticks and blocking the leg (3) using the top portion of the sticks where they are joined (the string end).

OPEN STICK BLOCK
(Outside of Leg)

Blocking from outside the opponent's kick (1-3) is also effective because this affords you greater protection than blocking inside the attacker's kick, where you are more vulnerable to a follow up strike, especially punches. Here you are forcing the direction of his attack, as well as his body, away from you. Use the string end of the nunchaku as before to make the block. Always be prepared to follow up with another strike to a vital area.

OPEN STICK BLOCK
(Top of Foot)

When your opponent tries to kick you, step back to give yourself distance from his kick (1-3) and execute a strong open stick snap block down on the top of his foot, using the string end of the sticks. Be prepared for a punch or other attack after the block. From this position, a strong follow up strike would be a thrust into his solar plexus using the same end of the sticks.

CLOSED STICK
SNAP BLOCK
(Against Punch)

(1) As your attacker throws a punch at you, step back or to the side away from his blow (2) and execute a strong snap strike (3) to his wrist. A strike directly on top of the wrist will cause your attacker a great deal of pain. Always keep your free hand high and close to your body, ready to block or push your opponent if needed.

OPEN STICK BLOCK
(Against Punch)

When your attacker is in close (1) and throws a punch at you (2), take a step back and open the nunchaku, raising it and then sweeping it down (3) on top of your attacker's incoming wrist. You are now able to grasp his wrist in an effective come-along hold, or deliver a two-stick strike to his solar plexus.

OPEN STICK BLOCK
(Against Punch)

This type of whip blocking allows fast, hard strikes without letting go of either nunchaku stick. (1) When you are threatened with a punch, grasp the stick in your right hand tightly, step back away from the force of the attack (2) and use the stick in the left hand like a club (3), striking your attacker's wrist. Always be prepared for a possible fake—the punch might suddenly become a groin kick or a foot sweep if you are not alert.

CLOSED STICK BLOCK
(Inside Elbow)

(1&2) If an attacker tries to strike you with his elbow, use the closed stick position to strike the inside of his arm (3) or a portion of his elbow. Be prepared for a counterstrike on the attacker's part, and to follow up with another strike. Use your free hand to support the block, ready to grab your opponent's wrist.

CLOSED STICK BLOCK
(Outside Elbow)

This block (1-3) may also be delivered to the outside of an attacker's elbow strike. Again, you have the option of hitting the arm directly or on the tip of the elbow. Be sure to step away from the force of the attack and keep your free hand high. From this angle, you are better able to deliver a follow up strike to the attacker's leg from the rear, knocking him down.

OPEN STICK BLOCK
(Against Elbow Strike to Ribs)

An open stick block, delivered downward (1-3) onto an attacker's elbow strike makes contact with both his upper arm and his forearm, and places the nunchaku in a perfect position for a control technique. Step back when you deliver these strikes, keeping yourself in a balanced position so you are better able to follow up with a control technique or another strike.

OPEN STICK BLOCK
(Against Upward Elbow Strike)

(1&2) If an attacker tries to elbow you in the face, use an open stick block to net the elbow (3) as it comes up, then sandwich the attacker's arm between the sticks and maintain a constant pressure until he is under control. Remember to step back and maintain a good, balanced position for more control and to protect your feet from sweeps that might knock you off balance. Twisting the sticks to either the right or left should take your attacker to the ground.

CLOSED STICK BLOCK
(Against Knife Hand Strike)

(1-3) A two-handed strike with the nunchaku in the closed position is a very good way to block a powerful knife hand strike. From this position, you may drop underneath his arm after your strike and deliver a follow up strike to his solar plexus or the side of the neck.

OPEN STICK BLOCK
(Against Knife Hand Strike)

(1&2) When your attacker throws a knife hand, step into a firm stance and use an open stick block (3) to catch his hand and wrist. You are now able to wrap the nunchaku quickly around his wrist and use a control technique to subdue him.

CLOSED STICK BLOCK
(Against Ridge Hand Strike)

(1&2) As your attacker throws a ridge hand strike toward your face, step back into a balanced position and, using both hands in the closed stick position, strike (3) upward to the attacker's forearm. Try to force his arm out away from you. Your opponent is now set up for a good counterstrike from the nunchaku. A neck hold from this position will drop your attacker to the ground.

OPEN STICK BLOCK
(Against Ridge
Hand Strike)

The open stick block (1-3) with the nunchaku against a ridge hand gives you the advantage of placing the attacker in a trapping, control technique. If you close the sticks quickly about his arm, he will be in too much pain to be able to follow up with a punch with his other arm or a kick. Always be careful of a secondary attack from your opponent.

CLOSED STICK BLOCK
(Against Hair Grab)

(1&2) If your attacker grabs your hair, don't panic. Drop your weight (3) and bring the closed nunchaku upward against the underside of his wrist. If you strike him hard enough he will have to let go.

OPEN STICK BLOCK
(Against Hair Grab)

An open stick technique against a hair grab is good too, but in this case you use the open sticks to wrap about the wrist of your attacker (1-3) and bring him down abruptly by crushing his wrist between the sticks. In this case, the weight is dropped and the shoulder turned, left hand over right, to twist the opponent's arm and force him down.

CLOSED STICK BLOCK
(Against Bo)

(1) When threatened with a side swipe from a bo, use the nunchaku in the closed stick position and block (2&3) the bo, deflecting it downward. Note the string end of the nunchaku is pointed down and is held in the hand farthest from the attack. If you can, reach out and grab the bo (4) to control the attack. Your nunchaku is in a position to be opened up into a strike to his groin or leg areas.

CLOSED STICK BLOCK
(Alternate)

(1-4) The same block and grab can be executed as before, but here you slide your right hand up to the ends of the sticks and then block downward (counterclockwise) to sweep the bo away. Notice how the nunchaku protects the right forearm. The block is just as effective, but a follow up strike from this position is more difficult.

SWING BLOCK
(Against Bo)

(1&2) An attack with a bo may also be deflected by a quick shoulder load snap strike. The right arm brings the nunchaku up, left hand underneath the right elbow gripping the lower stick, ready to block a high strike (3) or, as in this example, swing (4) at a low strike. The left hand releases the nunchaku as the right spins it down across the body to snap block the bo. Note the raised leg to prevent a strike to the ankle area.

OPEN STICK BLOCK
(Against Bo)

(1&2) When threatened with a bo attack, a two-handed, open stick block is excellent for parrying the bo strike (3&4) and forcing it down and away from your body. By extending the sticks at a 45-degree angle, you provide a greater area of coverage to meet the bo swing and protect yourself. With a quick flip of the wrist, you could deliver a snap strike to his legs or groin. Remember to shift away from his strike and maintain your feet in a wide stance.

OPEN STICK BLOCK
(Against Bo Jab)

(1) When your opponent threatens with a direct, forward poke to your abdomen with a bo, step back into a solid defensive stance and open the nunchaku (2), striking down onto the bo (3) and sweeping it aside with a circular motion. From this position you could conceiveably clasp the bo between the nunchaku and take it away from your opponent. An alternate method of blocking a forward poke would be with a closed stick snap strike, delivered in the opposite direction from your body's movement (see inset 3A); that is, as you step aside to the right to avoid the bo jab, you should block left, directing the bo even further away from you. You are now in a good position to deliver a snap strike to your attacker.

ALTERNATE

CLOSED STICK BLOCK
(Against Overhead Strike)

(1&2) When your opponent attempts an overhead strike, drop back into a strong stance and raise the nunchaku, closed stick, with both hands (3&4), blocking the bo. Overhead blocks can be tricky if your attacker is experienced, for he may try to swipe your side or strike the legs at the last moment. You must be prepared for any eventuality.

OPEN STICK BLOCK
(Against Overhead Strike)

(1) When your opponent tries an overhead strike, an open stick block may be used as well, stepping back as before (2) into the defensive posture, separating the sticks (3) and blocking the bo (4) with an upward motion, angling the sticks as shown in the inset (4A). The moment the bo strikes the weapon overhead, pull the sticks outward. (5&6) Here is the *incorrect* way to block an overhead strike. If you do

4A

4

5

not angle the nunchaku upward as in 4A then the force of the blow will not be stopped and the strike will drive into your head or face. If you do not step back away from the strike, you are also increasing the chances of being hit. At this point it is too late to reevaluate the block just executed. Remember: *never* step into a strike and always parry an overhead strike with the sticks angled *upward.*

6

OPEN STICK BLOCK
(Against Rear Attack)

This block involves throwing the weapon over the shoulder to block a strike aimed at your back, a move that requires a great deal of practice. When your opponent moves in behind you unexpectedly (1&2), use the hand farthest from the attacker to throw the nunchaku (3) over the same shoulder, catching it (4&5) behind your back with the opposite hand and clasping

the weapon tightly to stop the force of the blow. The advantage of this position is that you may now strike the opponent using either hand. The left hand in this example could swing the nunchaku low at the attacker's legs or up into his groin. The right hand could whip the nunchaku across and down for a strike to the attacker's upper body or head.

OPEN STICK BLOCK
(Against Bo)

Another way to stop a bo jab uses the same whip blocking technique. When you are threatened (1), take a step back and to the right, away from the force of the attack (2), maintaining a tight grip on the right hand stick. Raise the left hand stick simultaneously (3&4) for a whip strike at the bo. In this example, by stepping to the right, the defender is now able to aim a snap strike inside the attacker's vital areas, such as the groin and solar plexus.

OPEN STICK BLOCK
(Against Bo)

Almost identical to the previous whip block, only here the attacker's blow is deflected so that his back will be to you. The defender pivots to the left (1-4) and whips the right hand stick at the bo, and is now in good position to snap a strike at the attacker's lower leg or back.

FRONT LOAD BLOCK
(Left Side)

An overhead bo strike may also be parried with a block from the shoulder load position. (1&2) As your attacker moves in, separate the sticks and feed the left hand stick toward your right shoulder and inside your right arm, which will act as a support for your left elbow. The left hand stick now pro-

tects the forearm (3&4) and the right hand stick guards your side in case the attacker should swing the bo in that direction instead. You are now in a good position for a strike. Keep the nunchaku sticks at an angle roughly 45 to 90 degrees. Extend your left arm out fully.

SIDE LOAD BLOCK
(Against Bo)

The side load block affords a great deal of protection from a direct side attack. (1&2) When your opponent aims a high strike at your head or shoulder area, pivot to the right, planting your feet firmly and moving the left-hand stick up high and inside your right arm to (3&4) protect your head.

3

The right hand is underneath your left armpit, protecting the side. If your opponent had threatened you with an overhead strike as before but went for your ribs instead (see inset 4A), you would still be able to block as effectively using the side load block.

4

4A

OUTSIDE FOREARM BLOCK

This strong block will protect your forearm from injury. (1) If an opponent throws a knife hand strike, from a closed stick position turn your left hand around on top of the left-hand stick (2) and extend your left arm forward (3&4) underneath the right stick, while pulling the right

**FRONT VIEW
1**

**FRONT VIEW
2**

hand underneath your left elbow. Notice that the left-hand stick rests along the outside of your left fore-arm (see front views 1-4) protecting your arm and side while your right hand maintains a firm grasp on the other stick, ready to strike with if necessary.

**FRONT VIEW
3**

**FRONT VIEW
4**

OUTSIDE FOREARM BLOCK (Against Bo)

(1) When your opponent threatens you with a bo, step back (2) and raise the nunchaku as before, your left hand palm down, pulling the left-hand stick straight ahead (3) and across your forearm. Your right hand is palm up pulling the right-hand stick against your chest,

keeping the weapon taut. The overhead strike is blocked (4) by the extended, left-hand stick serving as a shield. Be sure to keep the nunchaku angled in order to deflect the bo strike off to the left of your shoulder. Be prepared for a follow up strike.

STRIKING

Outlined in this chapter are the most common vulnerable areas of an opponent's body that you can deliver strikes to with either an open or closed stick movement. Remember that any part of the nunchaku can be used effectively to strike someone: the open ends of the sticks for jabbing; the string end for poking; the closed position for striking, punching and jabbing; and the swinging motion for hitting with the ridged sides of the sticks.

This chapter shows only some of the possible areas you may strike; it does not show you *how* or *when* to strike. Striking drills and self-defense moves will describe *how* in a later chapter. *When* you should strike is never obvious, but you should always remember that it's better to wait until all other means of ending a confrontation peaceably have failed.

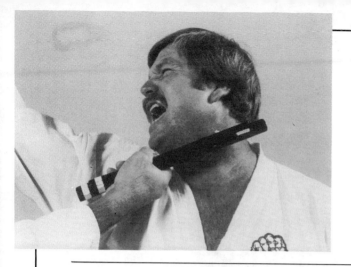

HORIZONTAL STRIKE

A short, closed stick strike for quick, interior movement. This strike to the neck is delivered horizontally, with a strong grip and the sticks are held close to the ends for more power.

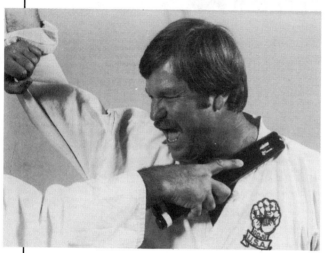

VERTICAL STRIKE

With a slight turn of the hand you may deliver a vertical strike to the clavicle or solar plexus. The forefinger of the striking hand is between the two sticks to strengthen delivery of the strike.

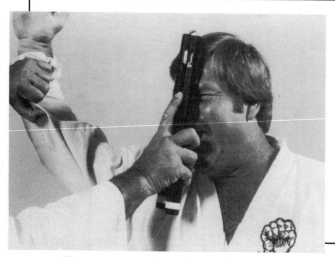

PUSH STRIKE TO FACE

The grip on the closed sticks is basically the same as with the vertical strike, though slightly higher near the center with the forefinger between the two sticks. This strike makes contact directly with the face and mouth. This strike is not advised for law enforcement.

HORIZONTAL PUSH STRIKE

You may also deliver this strike to the side of the face near the temple or ear. This particular strike, however, is to be used only in an extreme emergency, as it can cause serious damage to the person. This strike is not advised for law enforcement.

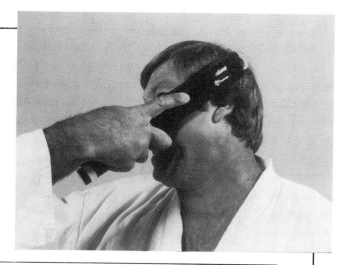

FORWARD POKE

This closed stick strike is also very dangerous to your opponent, and should be avoided. The blow is driven upward into the throat or base of the chin. This strike is not advised for law enforcement.

BACKHAND STRIKE

A strike delivered to the lower rib cage or the kidneys can be very effective. Use the open end of the sticks to strike with (string end opposite) and closed sticks for maximum punch. This strike can also be driven into the nerves of the armpit area.

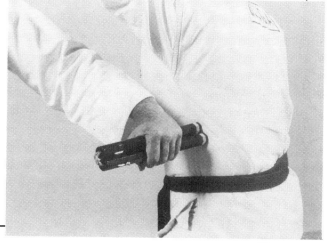

VERTICAL GROIN STRIKE

A closed stick attack to the groin will stop any attacker. This must be delivered quickly, and you must be on guard in case you have to block first.

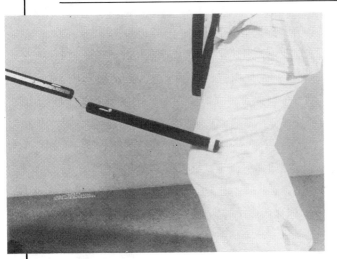

HORIZONTAL STRIKE
(Open Stick)

An open stick strike will give you more force when you hit an attacker than the closed stick position. You must remember that when you strike someone this way, however, the force of the stick's recoil can be directed at you just as quickly. This strike to the knee cap is a quick way to drop an opponent.

VERTICAL GROIN STRIKE
(Open Stick)

The striking area between your attacker's legs may not always be wide enough for you to apply an open stick strike, but if it is possible it should render your attacker helpless.

VERTICAL ELBOW STRIKE
(Open Stick)

A fast open strike to the elbow will force your attacker to release any grip he may have on you. A blow to his ulnar nerve (the "funny bone") underneath the elbow will deaden his entire arm.

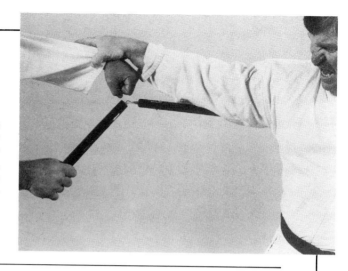

HORIZONTAL RIB STRIKE
(Open Stick)

Good as a primary or secondary (follow-up) strike. Impacting the ribs can drop an attacker easily. If the strike hits just slightly to the rear of his left side, you may even strike the spleen.

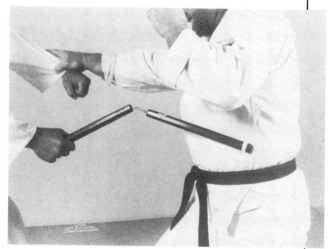

SOLAR PLEXUS STRIKE
(Open Stick)

Holding one stick in each hand, a forceful upward drive into the solar plexus can knock the air out of an attacker. Keep the weapon open and taut with a firm grip. Very good when your attacker is too close for a swing strike.

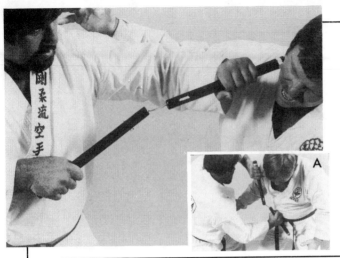

PUNCHING
(Open Stick)

Punching with the sticks in your hands, (but using the sticks for the impact) can be a very effective strike. This is good when you have a short time to react and your attacker is in close, yet the sticks will cause him much greater pain than your own hand. Demonstrated here are punches to the face and (see inset A) stomach.

LOW GROIN STRIKE
(Open Stick)

A strike to the groin area using the open stick method is effective if room does not allow a strike to the solar plexus.

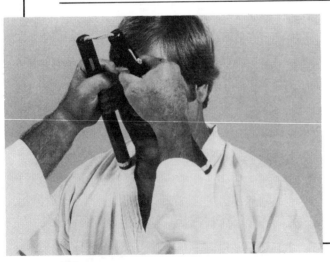

DOUBLE
OVERHEAD STRIKE
(Open Stick)

With this strike, you can attack both clavicle areas simultaneously. If your attacker is trying to grab you from the front, you can deliver this open stick blow, forcing the nuncha-ku downward onto his back.

SOLAR PLEXUS STRIKE
(String End)

From the same position as before, you can also drive the sticks upward by merely turning the sticks around, striking with the string end upward into the solar plexus or lower stomach.

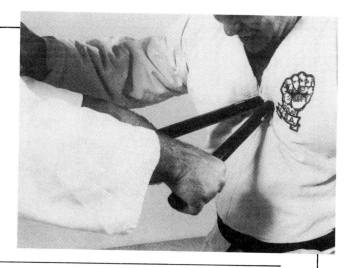

TRAP STRIKE
(Open Stick)

This is really a block and a strike. You bring the nunchaku down quickly to trap the attacking foot or arm, pinning the attacker between the two sticks.

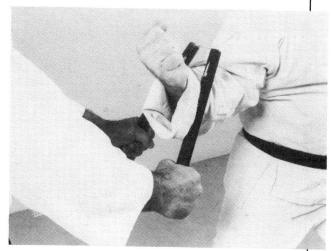

UPWARD TRAP STRIKE
(Open Stick)

The same method can apply when you are forcing an attacker's hand grab up and away from you. If you snap the nunchaku strongly enough, you will deaden the nerves in his hand and loosen his grip.

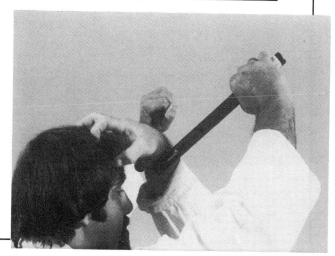

NUNCHAKU DRILLS

The following are more advanced nunchaku striking drills that are to be practiced over and over with the stick using both your strong and weak hands. The end of the weapon that is allowed to swing freely should be in constant motion. These drills will build up your speed and power in delivering the weapon open stick to specific areas of an opponent's body. The time listed in parenthesis next to each striking system is the time it should take the experienced student to execute all parts of the striking system.

When the striking systems are memorized, practice each of them on a "numb john" or other life-size practice dummy and try to execute each drill while hitting the dummy. Hit the targets continuously for one minute. As your proficiency increases you should be able to strike the dummy up to 120 times in one minute.

EIGHT-PART STRIKING SYSTEM
(Five Seconds)

Starting from the short guard (1) high point position, execute a vertical strike (2-6) upward and then down on the same side of your body. Follow with two horizontal strikes, one left (7-9) and then back to the right

4

2

3

6

7

Continued on next page

(10&11), never pausing between swings. Be sure you pass the nunchaku completely past your body both left and right at full speed. The fifth and sixth strikes in this system are two cross strikes, forming an "X" in mid-air. After the last horizontal strike the nunchaku is brought up (12) above and behind the right shoulder and swung down and across your body to the left (13&14) and below your waist. The next cross swing is executed the same way, from your

11

1

Continued on next page

shoulder to below the waist (15-17) moving from left to right. The seventh and eighth strikes are two revolutions about the head (18-21) in an overhead circular strike.

18

1A

1

FOUR-PART STRIKING SYSTEM
(Two Seconds)

(1) Assume the rear ready position. (Inset 1A shows how the weapon should be placed around the waist.) Using the right hand, release the nunchaku with your left hand and execute a swing strike from right to left (2-4) catching your opponent on his left shoulder and trapping the nunchaku (5) on the left side. The second strike comes off your hip (6-9) and

3

6

Continued on next page

9

12

back up above your right shoulder. Imagine that you are catching your opponent under the chin with this move. Now deliver the third strike down and across to the left side again (10&11) as if you were striking an opponent's clavicle and return to the left (12) side trap position. The last strike is delivered across from left to right and low, as if to the knee cap (13-15) and then returned to the original rear ready position (16&17).

15

10

11

13

14

16

17

This is a combined, seven-part blocking and striking drill. It should be performed with both the left and right hands (in this case, we use the right hand).

Note: The up and down swings of the vertical strikes and the side-to-side, left-to-right swings of the horizontal strikes each count as one part or strike/block of this drill.

SEVEN-PART BLOCKING AND STRIKING SYSTEM
(Four Seconds)

From a short guard high point position (1) step back with the right foot (2) and execute a strong, downward block. Now go immediately into a left side load block (3) and then shift to a right side load block (4-6). Now release the nunchaku with the left hand (7) and deliver a fast vertical strike over the right shoulder down (8-11)

Continued on next page

10

13

and then a vertical strike straight back up (12-15) and into the right side load position (16-18). When your left hand has caught the swinging nunchaku release it with your right hand

16

11

12

14

15

17

18

Continued on next page

(19) and deliver two fast horizontal strikes first from right to left (20-22) and then back from left to right (23-26). Catch the nunchaku in a right side trap position (27&28) and

Continued on next page

deliver an uppercut strike (make sure you have at least two inches of stick on the end to strike with) using the side load move (29-31) and then finish (32-36) with a circle or channel catch. The feet should close at the same time the stick is caught.

29

30

32

33

35

36

TRAP, LOAD AND STRIKE DRILL
(One Minute)

Begin from a short guard high point position (1) and execute a cross strike (2&3) down from the right shoulder to the left side and trapping it. Now execute a left side load block (4&5) and deliver a cross strike diagonally (6&7) from the left shoulder and

Continued on next page

7

trapping it on the right side. Load the nunchaku into a right side load position (8&9) and repeat the cross strike from right to left (10&11), trapping it on the left side (12) and repeating the next side load block and cross strike to return the nunchaku to the right side. Repeat the sequence, load block to cross strike to trap to load block to cross strike over and over until one minute is up.

10

8

9

11

12

THROWING DRILLS

Many instructors would not advocate throwing the nunchaku, but I recommend it for any police training for the simple reason that the nunchaku can be very effective in dropping someone if it is caught around their legs. London constables are trained how to throw their night sticks with excellent results.

Students can also learn how to toss the nunchaku to each other safely at distances of 15 to 20 feet. This has application in police work if a patrolman is without his nunchaku and his partner could throw it to him if he needed it in a tight situation.

Learning how to catch the nunchaku in flight, both open and closed stick, can also be an excellent training tool in just getting to know the capabilities of the nunchaku and its circular motions.

SHORT TOSS

For tossing a short distance, about ten to 15 feet, hold the sticks closed (1) near the open end, and prepare to toss them under hand (2) with the string end pointed up and toward the person you are throwing the nunchaku. Keep your forefinger directly in the middle between the two sticks. Toss (3) palm upward. The sticks should follow a straight flight pattern, and the sticks should now remain fairly close together or closed entirely. This will make them easier to catch.

RECEIVING THE SHORT TOSS

Preparing to catch the nunchaku thrown closed stick is fairly easy. Your partner should aim for the center of your body (1-3) and keep the weapon relatively low. It should travel

upward and you should be able to stand still (4&5) and receive it. Let the weapon come to you, don't try to snatch it out of the air.

THROWING—OPEN STICK

Hold the weapon (1) in a short guard high point position. Step back into a stable, wide stance (2) and load the weapon on the side, grasping each stick firmly. Your front hand will throw and guide the weapon in a straight flight. Keep your eyes on the target and throw the nunchaku (3&4)

with a smooth motion, releasing the weapon when your hand is pointed at your target. You must practice this frequently so that you will not throw the weapon too early or too late. Twenty-five yards is a good distance for this throw.

CATCHING—OPEN STICK

When you prepare to catch the weapon, remember that the open stick nunchaku is twirling through the air like a helicopter blade. Do not stand directly underneath it when you attempt to catch it. Try to let it drop into your open hand (1&2) to either side of your body. Reach for the middle of the sticks. The higher the throw, the easier it will be to catch. Practice throwing and catching the weapon with a partner standing about 20 feet apart.

TARGET THROWING

If you were throwing the nunchaku to drop someone, you would throw it low and with sufficient spin to strike them in the chest area or around the legs. Throw as before (1-3), extending the throwing arm toward the target and keeping it there until it has struck. In practice, you would use a striking dummy (*not* a real person). You should try to strike the practice dummy ten out of ten times, and practice throwing with both your strong and weak hands.

DEFENSES

T his chapter contains three distinct sections on self-defense using the nunchaku. The first deals with defenses against grabs, using swift strikes to stop the attack. The second details block-and-kick combinations; the third is on self-defense against a knife.

These are not the only methods of using the nunchaku, for its versatility makes a complete listing of every technique impossible. They are infinite.

The safest way to defend against a knife attack is with an open stick block and counter. This gives you a striking distance that is considerably safer, and you can generate great speed with the sticks for striking when they are open. It is better to try and strike your attacker's hand or wrist, rather than aiming for the weapon itself. You must strike quickly and retract the nunchaku for a follow up strike immediately. A blow to his knee cap or other sensitive area may be enough to drop his weapon.

When you are being attacked with a knife, always keep on the move so that you are never a standing target, facing your opponent straight on. When it comes to knife fighting you never know what your attacker's intention will be, whether he will deliver a stab or a slice. Always step away from him, never toward him. And never assume that he has only one weapon. Another knife may be concealed on his person.

When blocking a knife thrust, never maintain a straight line with the knife and your body. Always try to deflect the force and direction of the attack. Your arms must be locked if you intend to stop the force of his attack.

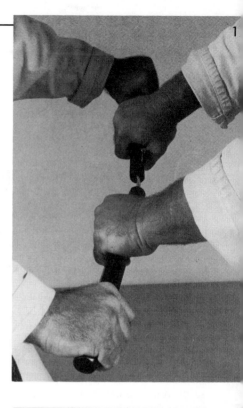

AGAINST STICK GRAB

(1) If your attacker reaches out and grabs your nunchaku inside of your own grasp, bring the ends of the weapon inward toward his hands (2-5), applying pressure like a vise until you capture his hands between the sticks and you will be able to control him. Notice that the hands are kept at the ends of the nunchaku for more leverage, and the hands rotate over the top so that your palms are now inward, exerting more force.

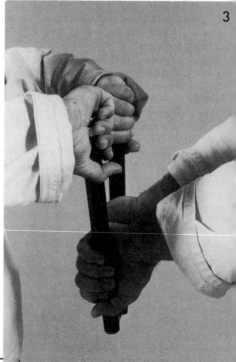

2

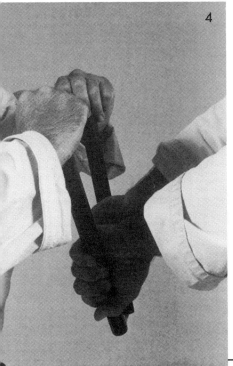

4

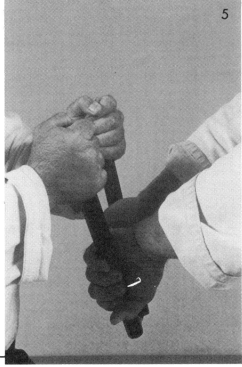

5

AGAINST ONE-HAND LAPEL GRAB

(1&2) Against a shoulder grasp, quickly flip the nunchaku stick over your opponent's wrist, catching the opposite stick in your free hand (3) and applying vise-like pressure (4) to remove your attacker's hand. Spin his hand and body away from you. If you apply a sufficient

amount of pressure your opponent will be in too much pain to counter with a punch or kicking motion. It is important to apply the squeeze to the wrist and not the upper arm, because the wrist area is far more sensitive to pressure on the nerve endings.

AGAINST TWO-HAND LAPEL GRAB

The same maneuver is perfect for a two-hand grab. (1) If your collar is grabbed, flip the sticks over his arms (2&3) and catch it in your free hand, closing the sticks quickly together and removing (4&5) his hands easily as you squeeze his wrists together. Prepare to step

backward toward your strong side, moving away from his attack and leaving as much room as possible. If you are maintaining a strong, tight squeeze on his wrists, forcing them down and away, you should have no problem controlling him.

AGAINST CHOKE HOLD

This is a quick way to stop a bear hug or choke hold. (1) When your attacker makes his move, place the string end of the closed stick nunchaku in the palm of your weak hand (2) and pivot them so that the open ends are now facing your opponent (3). Pull the

sticks apart and deliver a strong strike (4) into the center of his armpits. Your grasp should be firm, with thumbs on top of the sticks. Make sure your weight is dropped and your stance strong to give you added force to your delivery.

AGAINST CHOKE HOLD

One example of employing an open stick strike from a closed stick ready position is when your attacker catches you off guard. (1) Step backward and drop your weight (2&3) to try

and pull him off balance, simultaneously opening the nunchaku and striking (4) up into the solar plexus. A follow-up strike to the groin or chin may be necessary.

AGAINST CHOKE HOLD

(1) If your attacker grabs you in a choke hold, you can stun him with an open stick drive to the solar plexus (2&3) and then deliver a closed stick snap strike (4&5) to the side of his neck. The free hand should always be prepared to counter or shove your opponent if needed. Step further away from the momentum of your opponent and deliver an open stick strike (6-8) to his knee to drop him.

AGAINST BEAR HUG

This will stop an attacker from placing you in a bear hug from the front. From a high point short guard position (1), with the string end on top, lift the nunchaku over your head (2&3) spreading the sticks apart so that you can deliver a strong, double

strike (4) directly into his clavicle on either side of his neck. A strong blow will stop him immediately. Your grasp should be near the center of each stick. If he drops and tries to tackle you, a double strike to the center of his back will stop him.

AGAINST REAR ATTACK

(1) If you are grabbed from behind, instantly take a deep breath and force your arms backward (2) and your body forward. Then you must throw your buttocks and lower abdomen backward (3) as forcefully as possible and throw your arms forward in an attempt to break his

hold. If you explode fast enough, you may have knocked the wind out of him and you will be able to strike him quickly. When you are free (4), step forward into a strong ready position and flip the nunchaku (5) into an open strike to his knee (6) or the closest vulnerable spot.

AGAINST REAR ATTACK

(1) If you are seized or choked from behind, step forward (2) with your right (or strong) foot and grasp one end of the nunchaku in your left hand (3) so that you grasp it with a reverse palm grip. Now you are ready to pivot (4&5) to the left and push his left arm away from your neck by applying a sweeping forearm block. Now that you have an open "strike lane" you can deliver a punch (6-8) to his face using the weapon. A series of secondary strikes may be delivered at this point.

2

4

5

7

8

AGAINST HEADLOCK

(1) If you are caught in a head lock, lift your nunchaku over his head (2) and smash it upward under his nose and (3&4) si-

multaneously grabbing or hitting his groin. Keep applying pressure up and back and you will force him off balance.

AGAINST HEADLOCK

If your nunchaku is in the hand behind your opponent's body (1) transfer it to your front hand and quickly use the closest stick with a direct upward thrust to his groin (2&3) using the string end. Your

right hand can reach over his holding arm and deliver a palm smash (4) to his face. When you are able to move away from him, follow up with a secondary strike to any vulnerable spot.

AGAINST HEADLOCK

An alternate method of loosening a head grab (1) is to open the nunchaku up and catch it (2&3) between the opponent's legs with the hand behind his back. With a firm grasp on

each end lift up (4) as hard as you can. This should upset his balance enough that you can escape his hold and deliver a quick secondary strike.

AGAINST PUNCH

One good technique to follow through with after you deliver a closed stick block to an opponent's punch (1-3) is to grab the attacker's sleeve (4) while

still grasping the nunchaku and deliver a knee kick to his ribs or solar plexus (5) while he is off balance.

AGAINST KNIFE HAND

(1-3) Your opponent throws a knife hand at you and you respond with an open stick block to his wrist. If you are going to counter with a groin kick, it must be delivered fast and hard (4) if you are not to be taken off balance. Always give priority to the block—the kick is secondary. Do not

drop the block until the kick has driven the attacker back or to the ground. A kick may also be driven into his solar plexus. If you choose to deliver a kick to the opponent's face, remember that this is your weakest position and may leave you open to a foot sweep.

AGAINST KNIFE HAND

The quickest kick that you can deliver from either a frontal or side position is the side kick. When your opponent throws a knife hand (1-3), you block with

the open stick and, while maintaining the block (4), use the side of the foot to strike the knee or lower leg area.

AGAINST KNIFE HAND

(1) From the closed stick ready position, you can block a knife hand strike with the same open stick block (2&3), and respond with a side kick (4) to the rib cage or solar plexus.

The kick must snap out and back or your opponent, if not sufficiently damaged, may grab your foot and take you to the ground.

AGAINST BO

When caught in a position where you must protect yourself while your back is to your opponent (1), you can execute an effective rear block by raising the nunchaku, open stick (2-4), to meet the attacker's weapon. Always try to maintain a balanced

stance by keeping your feet apart. By dropping your weight a bit and turning slightly you can deliver a strong back kick (5&6) to the groin, solar plexus or knee cap. But make sure you have blocked first, then concern yourself with a counterstrike.

AGAINST BO

(1-3) Should it become necessary to defend yourself from the ground, make sure you have a set fighting procedure to follow for this type of sparring. Remember that the block is always of primary importance and the kick or follow up is secondary. Here, the attacker's bo strike is blocked with the

open stick position (4), and the legs are used to kick the knee and to push the attacker (5&6) to the ground. You should try to regain your feet as fast as you can if you are knocked down. If you have no formal training in these kinds of situations, do so before you have to in a real live situation.

AGAINST SHOULDER GRAB

When confronted with a much bigger opponent, you may want to catch him off guard. (1) If your attacker moves in on you turn toward your strongest side (2&3), trying to keep your distance and keeping the weapon ready. (4-6) Snap the nunchaku (closed stick) at the side of his face. At the moment of impact, your body should still be twisted, your legs flexed and your blow traveling backward. Once he has been stunned, deliver a strong back or side kick (7&8) to his stomach. When you practice this technique, be sure to try both sides of your body, especially your weak hand, and try kicking with one foot and then the other.

AGAINST KNIFE

(1) Against an upper body stab, step back into a good defensive stance (2), opening the nunchaku and bracing for an upward block (3) against the knife. Staying to the outside of the attacker's knife hand, quickly bring the right hand with the nunchaku

stick over the attacker's arm (4) and pressing his arm down and away (5) from your body. Squeeze the nunchaku (6) continually until he drops the weapon in pain. Be careful that he does not try a foot sweep or punch with his left hand.

AGAINST KNIFE

(1) If your attacker lunges straight in at you and you are in the short guard position, make sure you step back (2&3) as you separate the nunchaku for a quick parry downward, striking the wrist of the knife hand (4) with the string end and quickly

clamping his wrist (5&6) and forcing it down and away from your body until he releases the weapon in pain. The thumbs are on top of both sticks pushing downward. You should follow immediately with a strike.

TAKEDOWN TECHNIQUES

Even better than blocking an opponent's strike is to convert that block into a takedown technique which will force the attacker off balance and bring him to the ground where he will be unable to attack you anymore. These techniques are harder to learn than just blocking, and require plenty of practice to master. Remember as you execute each one that you should maintain a good balanced stance by stepping back away from the attack and planting both feet firmly but flexibly so that you can block properly and convert the attacker's force of attack against him.

TAKEDOWN #1

(1&2) From a high point position, your assailant throws a punch at you. Execute a snap block (3&4) and move to the outside of his punch simultaneously. Your block should then feed over his arm and shoulder (5-7) placing you behind him with the closed nunchaku firmly around his neck. Use your right foot now to stamp the back of his knee (8) or lower leg and force him to the ground. Law enforcement officers should place the weapon only on the side of the neck.

183

TAKEDOWN #2

(1&2) Should your attacker reach out and grasp your collar, throw the nunchaku over the top of his forearm (3), catching the opposite stick in your free hand and applying pressure inward and down (4), pinning his arm painfully and forcing him into a crouched position. You can now execute a swift front kick (5) to his groin. Now raise the sticks together (6&7) and deliver a follow up strike to the back of his shoulder. This will prevent him from trying to tackle you and taking you down with him. Another strike (8&9) may be necessary if this is not enough. By keeping the sticks separated, you strike two areas at the same time. You are also prepared to place the nunchaku about his neck.

TAKEDOWN #3

(1-3) An alternate method of defending against a kick is by trapping the opponent's foot from underneath as he raises his leg. The sticks are brought up underneath his heel and follow the leg's upward motion, pulling him

(4) off balance. If you have a firm grip on both sticks and don't let up you can crush the ankle bone. The main object is to keep his foot from striking you. It takes a great deal of practice to execute this trap block correctly.

TAKEDOWN #4

(1-3) Another method of breaking a shoulder or collar grasp is to follow the same motion, dropping your weight and bringing the nunchaku over his forearm. But this time you will throw the weapon from your left shoulder toward the middle of your body. Pivot to your right (if

3

4

that is your strongest side) and trap his arm (4) between the nunchaku sticks. Your elbow over the top of his arm puts more pressure on his upper torso. By continuing this twisting motion (5) you should force him down. This technique is known as an arm bar.

5

TAKEDOWN #5

(1) When you must react quickly to a sudden inside punch or strike, block upward (2) using the open stick technique and begin to move *into* his attacking arm. Your right hand brings the nunchaku around his forearm (3) and then the sticks are closed together quickly, forcing

his right hand backward. Notice how the stick in the right hand is crossing his forearm providing leverage for the twist at the elbow. You are forcing his wrist back toward his elbow on top of the stick. This technique (4-6) will drop him quickly.

6

TAKEDOWN #6

(1&2) When your attacker attempts a front kick to your midsection, step to the outside and at the same moment try to thread the closed stick nunchaku (3) underneath his ankle or at least near the bottom of his foot. With a continuous lifting motion (4&5) move into his body and grab his left shoulder with your left hand. Execute a left sweep to the back of his only supporting foot (6) and drive him down. When he is on the ground, you can deliver (7&8) a follow up strike to his rib cage.

TAKEDOWN #7

(1&2) A good method of taking your attacker down from a sudden punch is with an open stick block directed to the inside (3) of his body. At the moment of the block, step inward (4) toward his center and hit his chest with your right shoulder, whipping the nunchaku over the top of his head (5&6) onto his neck when you make contact. Always be alert at this point, as he could strike you in the groin with his right hand. With your pressure forcing his head down and a quick step back between his legs, drop your weight and throw him to the ground (7&8) over your right shoulder.

TAKEDOWN #8

This technique is excellent but must be practiced many times over before it can be perfected with the necessary speed. The attacker's punch (1-3) is blocked with a two-handed closed stick block. After you execute the block, grab his right wrist (4) with your left hand and turn the nunchaku on its side preparing to strike

him in his right rib area. Use only the last inch or so of the closed nunchaku (5) to strike with. If you hit him in the liver or kidneys, this should drop him immediately. When you strike do not let go of his right hand. Retract the weapon about ten inches from his body (6) and pull his arm toward you so he is off balance. Throw the

Continued on next page

197

7

8

weapon open stick over his left shoulder (7-9) and reach across the front of his neck with your free (left) hand to catch the other end. Force your left elbow into his throat (see inset A) and start to pivot to the left (10) making sure you keep a tight grip on

9

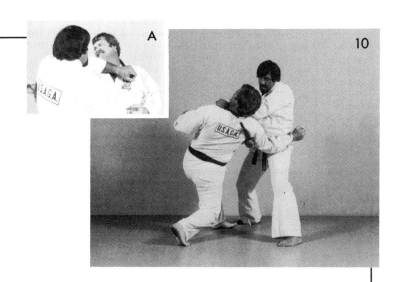

A

10

the weapon. Continue applying pressure to his shoulder and clavicle. With a constant pull on his neck you should be able to pivot and force him (11&12) to the ground. Use a follow up strike if necessary.

11

12

OUTDOOR TRAINING

This section is unique to nunchaku training, as it specifies a regimen of training/workout with the weapon that instructors can use, or a student can follow himself, that will improve his coordination and execution. Think of these movements as a form of kata, where the focus of your attention is on the weapon and nothing else. Perform each strike or blocking motion at least 100 times, and concentrate your attention on the motion, timing your breathing with the snap of the block or strike.

Instructors who are calling these movements should never cut the workout session short. By not working your students and belts to their maximum, you are not allowing them to develop to their maximum potential. Be critical of the slightest deviations from proper form in weapon handling and body position. They will be on their toes constantly and more appreciative if you are critical now rather than when they really need the training.

Before beginning these series of movements, a period of meditation should be set aside so that all distracting thoughts or problems from the day can flow out of the mind and nothing but the training flows in. If you are not mentally prepared, you will lose at least 50 percent of the total value of this workout. The workout should be conducted outdoors, since from day to day the weather will prove colder or warmer, giving the student a chance to adapt to strenuous exercise in varying conditions, sometimes uncomfortable. But stress on a hot day or a slightly chilly morning is good for conditioning.

SUMMARY OF WORKOUT ROUTINE

1. Meditation
2. Closed Stick Ready Position
3. Front Load Ready Position
4. Closed Stick Blocks (Low and High)
5. Closed Stick Blocks (Left and Right)
6. Closed Stick Blocks (Crouching and Standing)
7. Open Stick Blocks (Low and High)
8. Open Stick Blocks (Left and Right)
9. Side Load Blocks (Left and Right)
10. Forearm Blocks (Left and Right)
11. Blocking and Kicking
12. Closed Stick Pokes
13. Overhead Strikes
14. Circular Strikes
15. Debriefing

THE WORKOUT

(1) Preparing for a hard workout is just as important as the workout itself. A period of quiet meditation to eliminate distracting problems and thoughts is appropriate. (2) Assume the closed stick ready position before the execution of the techniques. The left hand is held behind the back, the right hand is extended in front of the body, forefinger between the middle of the sticks. Feet are in a wide stance, a little wider than shoulder width. (3) As-

sume the front ready position. Students should hold this stance and hold the nunchaku out in front of their body for five full minutes. From this position, block to the sides and overhead and then return to this position. (4) Execute a low closed stick block, both hands holding the nunchaku tightly, thrusting down with a snap. (5) Now execute a closed stick block overhead, watching for firm grip and stable balance. (6&7) From the overhead

Continued on next page

strike position, shift your weight to your front foot and turn your hips to deliver a closed stick side block, first to the left, then pivot and shift your weight to your other foot, blocking to the right side. Notice that when blocking to the left, the left hand is low for support, the right hand high. When blocking to the right, the right hand is low for support and the left hand is high. (8&9) Now step forward into a closed stick block using only one hand, from both the crouched and standing positions. In the crouched position, shift from foot to foot to strengthen the legs. Or try executing a forward roll on the shoulder and re-

turning to the crouched, blocking position. Standing, the open hand is used to block low, and the sticks are held at an angle for deflection. (10&11) Now execute open stick blocks, both high and low, with a strong stance by stepping back and snapping out, thumbs locked on top. You should be prepared to follow up quickly with a thrust or striking motion. Keep your weight low so that you are not locked into a particular stance and be ready to move about quickly. (12) The open stick block, right hand high, affords protection both from a punch or stick strike to your left, or a possible blow from the right side to your head.

Continued on next page

13

14

15

(13) The same open stick block to the left can be executed with the left hand high. It can be used as a sweep block, but it does not protect your right side. Both are executed from the front ready position. (14) The side load block, which can protect two areas, the head and side, simultaneously. Keep the sticks at this angle for deflecting blows. Otherwise, a strong strike could force your own sticks to hit you. Start from an open stick front ready position and move into the side block as fast as you can. Try it with the eyes closed, switching sides and repeating the drill over and over, or try for a time of

five blocks in ten seconds. (15) Execute the forearm block, where the left hand reverses its grip on the stick and brings it under the right wrist, and the right hand draws the other stick firmly across the left forearm and down the crook of the left elbow. The cat stance is appropriate for this block. (16) Assume a one leg stance held for eight to ten seconds while maintaining the front open stick position. Execute a side kick (17) ten times in a row without bringing your kicking foot to the ground. Form and balance should not be affected while practicing. (18) From the side kick move to a front kick

Continued on next page

(19) and maintain the front open stick position without losing balance. This will improve your balance and strengthen your kicks. (20) Execute a closed stick strike, using the string end to poke, forefinger along the middle of the sticks for support. Your free hand is low to block or push away your opponent. (21) Deliver a closed stick strike sideways (horizontal), string end forward as in figure 20. The free hand is held over head to protect the face. (22) Deliver an overhead strike, using the ends of each stick, driven down with a tight grip. Try

executing this drill with different feet forward, pivoting left and right quickly. (23) Now assume the underarm ready position with the nunchaku held under the armpit, opposite hand high for blocking. The right leg is back when the nunchaku is held in the right hand. (24) The nunchaku should never touch the ground at anytime during the workout. Always have the weapon where you can put it in action at anytime. Students can discuss what areas they need to improve on when cooling down from this training session.

ATTACK DRILLS

In this chapter are several drills that you can practice with a partner to increase your reflexes and improve your ability to respond quickly to a threatening situation. In all your practice with the nunchaku, always strive for realism. You cannot depend on the nunchaku or any other weapon, for that matter, if you ignore the importance of practice, timing, etc. One can never be too proficient in the use of his tools, be they for work, sport or self-defense. If you treat the nunchaku with respect, it can be a most capable and effective weapon.

ATTACK DRILL #1

Working with a partner, have him throw a right punch to your face (1&2) as you stand in the short guard high point position. As he steps in, step back (3) and execute an open hand/closed stick combination block. Before going on to the next attack, repeat this punch-and-block

drill with your partner, changing the speed at which he punches, watching for weaknesses on your part. Now have your partner step in (4&5) with a left face punch. Block it in the same manner, stepping back into a solid stance and blocking with both the free hand and the closed

Continued on next page

sticks. Combine the right and left punches now, always stepping back and blocking, one after the other, and have your partner speed up his punches. The next move is to grasp his left hand in your left hand after you block it (6) and pull him forward (7) off balance, raising your clos-

ed nunchaku and striking him (8) in the side of the neck or on top of the shoulder. Follow up with an open stick strike (9&10) to the leg area. Add these last attacks to the entire drill and repeat. When you have done it ten times, have your partner practice on you.

ATTACK DRILL #2

(1) From a ready position, have your partner reach out with either hand and grab you (2) on the wrist. If he grabs your right wrist, place the nunchaku over his wrist or forearm (3&4) by rotating your right wrist so that you bring the weapon over the outside

of his grasp and pull it on top of his wrist using your left hand. Press down (5&6) and bring him toward the ground. Once he is off balance, you can take the weapon in your free right hand (7&8) and strike his forearm or elbow.

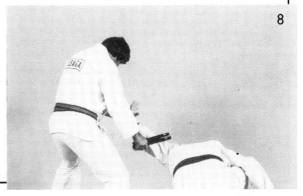

ATTACK DRILL #3

An alternate method of freeing your wrist (1&2) is to turn the weapon up so the string end is high on the inside of your partner's forearm and to reach under with your free hand (3) and grasp it (4), yanking it down

over his wrist (5) and forcing him to let go. Now pin his wrist with your left hand (6) and take the weapon in your right, delivering a closed stick strike (7) to the small of his back.

ATTACK DRILL #4

(1) If your partner grabs your closed stick in the middle instead of your wrist, step back and raise the sticks quickly (2), rotating the sticks by pulling down with the left hand

and pushing up with the right so that you force the sticks against his wrist (3), causing him pain. Lift up on his wrist when he lets go (4) and deliver a good strike (5) to the groin.

GLOSSARY

ARM BAR A technique where the attacker is controlled by exerting pressure with one or both sticks against the back of the elbow joint, forcing the attacker downward.

BO A long wooden staff; like the nunchaku, a kobudo weapon used during the feudal periods of Japanese and Okinawan history, circa A.D. 1400.

CENTRIFUGAL FORCE The force the nunchaku exerts while moving in a circular path away from the center of rotation; that is, as the weapon is circled over the shoulder the speed of the sticks is greater at the outside of the circle than in the center.

CHANNEL CATCH Stopping the swinging motion of the nunchaku by catching the free end with the same hand that grips the weapon. The stick is brought back with a snap between the thumb and forefinger (the channel area). Pressure is applied with the insides of both fingers to hold both sticks.

CHUCKS Slang for nunchaku.

CIRCLE STRIKES Any strike executed in a circular motion (for example, underarm strikes, overhead circle strikes).

CLOSED STICK Any position or technique where the weapon remains closed; that is, sticks together, held tightly in one or both hands.

COME ALONG Any hold that exerts enough painful pressure on an attacker to force him to "come along" with you peaceably.

CROSS X STRIKE Striking in a cross or "X" pattern directly in front of your body, with sticks either open or closed (usually open).

DOUBLE STRIKE Using the open end of the nunchaku sticks to deliver either a quick upward blow to the trunk or armpits or a quick downward blow onto the back or collar bone.

FOLLOW UP OR SECONDARY STRIKE Any strike used after the initial strike delivered to vulnerable areas of the body.

FOREARM BLOCK Placing the nunchaku, open stick, in a front position where one stick covers and protects the leading forearm against blows.

FRONT CATCH A combination strike and catch. Following an open stick strike, the free end of the weapon is caught underneath the armpit with the free hand.

FRONT LOAD A ready position, with the sticks held open and near the bottom about chest-high. The sticks form an upside-down "V" shape.

FRONT LOAD BLOCK When the front load position is used to block a direct assault to the body from the front.

HIGH POINT POSITION A closed stick ready position where the nunchaku is held with both hands and kept high in front of the chest area.

HORIZONTAL STRIKE	Any strike, either closed or open stick, delivered along a horizontal plane.
LOW POINT POSITION	A closed stick ready position where the nunchaku is held low along the side of the hip in either the left or right hand.
NUMB JOHN	A heavy, practice dummy approximating a man's shape used for striking drills.
NUNCHAKU	Two wooden sticks, usually 14 inches in length, bound together by a single cord or chain; a kobudo weapon from the feudal period of Japanese and Okinawan history.
OPEN END	The ends of the nunchaku not joined by the cord or chain. The ends can be held for blocking and striking and easily transferred from hand to hand.
OPEN STICK	Any position or technique where the weapon is fully extended to afford maximum distance for blocking and swing strikes. One stick is held while the other is allowed to swing freely.
OUTDOOR TRAINING	A practice session of drills with the nunchaku performed out of doors to adjust to working with the weapon under both hot and cold weather conditions.
POKE	A blow delivered to an attacker's vulnerable areas with a quick snap and recovery motion, usually forcing your attacker backward.
PUNCHING	Using the sticks, open or closed, in the same fashion as throwing a punch. The only difference is that the weapon makes the strike instead of the hand.
PUSH STRIKE	Using the sticks, closed or open, to force your attacker back by pushing (rather than poking) the weapon into the groin, chest or other vulnerable area.
REAR CATCH	Stopping an open stick swing strike by placing the catch hand in the small of the back to receive the free end of the weapon behind you.
RIDGES	The edges of a ridged nunchaku that form straight lines running up the length of each stick; useful for exerting pain on bony areas in a come along hold.
SHORT GUARD POSITION	Any closed stick ready position.
SHOULDER LOAD	An open stick ready position where the weapon is held at a 45-to 90-degree angle, one stick protecting the head area, the other stick the shoulder and rib cage area. The point where the sticks are joined rests on the top of the shoulder.
SHOULDER LOAD BLOCK	A side load used to block an attack. (If protecting the right side, the left hand holds one stick underneath the right armpit in a vertical position, while the right hand is held above the right shoulder grasping the other stick.

SIDE TRAP	Catching an open stick swing strike by trapping it against the opposite hip with the free hand on that side of the body. (For example, the right hand strikes across at the waist and the free end is trapped on the left hip with your left hand.)
SNAP BLOCK	Any quick motion with the sticks, open or closed, executing a block and then recovering the weapon quickly.
SNAP STRIKE	Any quick movement of the sticks, open or closed, striking a vulnerable area and then recovering the weapon quickly.
STRIKE LANE	The imaginary path the nunchaku follows toward a target.
STRIKING SYSTEM	The complete range of open and closed stick striking motions and combinations, including cross X, vertical, horizontal and overhead strikes.
STRING OR CORD	The universal joint of the nunchaku which connects the two sticks, allowing the sticks to move 360 degrees.
STRING END	The end of the sticks where the tops of the weapon are joined together. This end can be used for striking the solar plexus, groin, throat and other vulnerable areas.
STRONG HAND	The hand used most often for any task. The right hand is the strong hand for a right-handed person.
SWING STRIKE	Using the nunchaku open stick with the arm completely extended for a strike aimed at maximum distance away from the defender.
TAKEDOWN	Any technique which upsets an attacker's balance and forces him to the ground. A takedown can usually be followed immediately with a secondary strike or come along hold.
TRAP STRIKE	A strike executed from the side trap position by removing the trap hand to uncover the weapon.
VERTICAL STRIKE	A closed or open stick strike delivered along a vertical plane.
WEAK HAND	The hand that is seldom used for any tasks and with less confidence. In a right-handed person, his left hand would be his weak hand. All nunchaku techniques should be practiced with the weak hand as well as with the strong hand.